Harrison Moore

CREDIT SCORE

SECRETS

Learn How To Fix, Repair and Raise Your Credit Score Quickly and Get Rid of Bad Credit

Copyright © 2020 publishing.

All rights reserved.

Author: Harrison Moore

No part of this publication may be reproduced, distributed or transmitted in any form or by any means, including photocopying recording or other electronic or mechanical methods or by any information storage and retrieval system without the prior written permission of the publisher, except in the case of brief quotation embodies in critical reviews and certain other non-commercial uses permitted by copyright law.

Table of Contents

Chapter One 5
    What Your Credit Score Really Means 5
    High Credit Score Secrets.. 9
    What Does Credit Score Account For? 12
    Debt to Credit Ratios 16
    Do It Yourself Credit Score Repair 19

Chapter Two 22
    Credit Scoring and Your Financial History 22
    Credit Reporting and How Your Credit Score is Determined 25
    Build Credit History 30
    Build Credit Score Secrets.. 33
    Secrets to Building a High Credit Score 36
    Easy Steps to a Better Credit Score 38
    Top 5 Credit Score Myths... 43
    Raise Your Credit Score in a Flash 48

Chapter Four 51
    Repairing Your Credit Score 51
    How to Improve Your Credit Score Fast With These Secrets!... 55
    Surefire Ways to Repair a Bad Credit Score 60
    Credit Score Rating System... 63

Chapter Five 69
    Benefits of Good Credit 69

Is Good Credit Really Worth the Effort? 72

Maintaining Good Credit After Bankruptcy 76

The Advantages of Having a Good Credit Score 80

Chapter Six 83

A Good Credit Score Means More Than Just Getting a Loan
.... 83

Why Bad Credit Lenders Will Need to Adjust What is
Considered Good Credit 88

How One Good Credit Consultation Can Save a Life 91

Mistakes To Avoid To Maintain Good Credit Score 95

Ways That a Good Credit Repair Service Can Help Your
Situation 99

Chapter Seven 102

How to Rebuild a Good Credit History 102

Rebuild & Keep Good Credit Ratings by Understanding
Your Credit Cards 105

How to Qualify For and Establish Good Credit 116

Benefits of Improving Credit Report Scores 120

Chapter Eight 123

Enjoy The Benefits Of A Credit Card!! 123

Making a Good Credit Card Comparison 126

The Benefits Of Accessing Credit Reports On A Regular
Basis 130

Rebuild Your Credit With A Prepaid Credit Card 133

Help Find The Best Credit Cards Rates By Researching
Credit Cards Comparison 141

Is it Possible to Improve Your Credit Scores and Live a
Normal Life? 145

Chapter One

What Your Credit Score Really Means

There is a wide range of inquiries encompasses the to some degree strange credit score. That secret is made, to a limited extent, by the very offices who decide the number. Recipes for calculating the scores have stayed quiet, and the numbers are not promptly accessible; at any rate not without accomplishing some work to get them. Individuals frequently need to comprehend what precisely a credit score is, who is behind it, what things sway your rating, and what impact a credit score can have on day by day life. Add to that the intense monetary occasions we're currently in, and your credit rating turns out to be a higher priority than any time in recent memory. We should investigate what a credit score is and how it influences you.

A credit score is simply an endeavor to rank your creditworthiness with a goal number. It used to be that in the event that you needed a credit you would go into the bank, and in the event that you had a decent remaining in the network, or if the advance official had a positive sentiment about you, you could get an advance. Clearly, there is a blemish in that framework; anyone, regardless of how very much regarded, can be an awful credit hazard. Along these lines, by computing the impact of various factors on your capacity to reimburse, the credit offices concocted a way that tries to treat everyone decently.

There are a few distinct things considered by the credit offices when making sense of a score. Fortunately, a large portion of them is good judgment. The one thing that makes up the majority of your score is your installment history. Along these lines, probably the best thing you can begin doing (or keep doing) is taken care of the entirety of your tabs on schedule. Next, don't owe excessively. Your obligation to-salary proportion ought to be at 25% or less. That implies the sum you owe ought not to surpass 25% of your pay. Try not to open such a large number of records in a brief timeframe, and don't lose an excessive amount of either. Possibly apply for an advance or credit in the event that you genuinely need it. As referenced, a large portion of these things are sound judgment, and they will consistently go far towards improving your general budgetary wellbeing.

Is a credit score actually that significant, all things considered, it's just a number, isn't that so? Right, however, it's an inescapable number at that. The most notable model is the banks. They will utilize your credit score to decide if you get an advance, and assuming this is the case, what terms you will get. Be that as it may, your credit score is utilized by much something other than moneylenders. On the off chance that you go after a position, your potential business may pull your credit report before settling on their employing choice. Proprietors use credit scores to see who they will lease to. Insurance agencies use them as a component of their hazard evaluation before offering you an arrangement.

There is no uncertainty that your credit score is significant. Since you have more data on what it's everything about, you can find a way to maintain or improve your score.

High Credit Score Secrets

There are many advantages to a high credit score that can make life hassle free, but for those who don't have a great credit, fixing is really not a problem. It usually isn't until someone desperately needs a loan or is having trouble finding an apartment that they realize just how important it is to maintain a high credit score. And who would have known that silly late fee at the library had such a affect on your rating?

Good credit will help you quickly secure an auto loan, cash advance or an increased credit limit without hassle. A good score also shows a sense of being able to manage responsibility and make wise decisions in your life. For that reason, your credit score is often used during job interviews, getting car insurance, and even when trying to get new cell phone service.

While a couple relatively small mistakes can drive down you score and prevent you from getting what you need, bouncing back is an easy task. For the do-it-yourself individual, just an hour of cleaning your credit can boost your score as much as a couple hundred points. The results are not only the ability to secure a loan, but to also get an incredible rate that can save your thousands of dollars.

So how do you do it? The secret to having a high credit score is simple. It starts with understanding exactly how this score is calculated. When you know the five things that have the greatest impact on your score, you can manipulate this system in your favor to instantly give yourself a high credit rating.

One example of this is to reduce your debt utilization, which can account for as much as 25 percent of your score. If you are currently using more than half the available credit that has been extended to you, your score will suffer. In other words, if your $5,000 credit card limit currently has a $2,500 balance, the quickest way to boost your score is to reduce that balance.

This can be done be transferring some of that balance to another card in order to distribute your debt more evenly. Another way to accomplish this is to ask for a increase on your spending limit. Both can instantly reduce your debt utilization and raise your credit score.

What Does Credit Score Account For?

Any credit you have will be a piece of your credit report. This incorporates credit cards, vehicle advances, home loans and understudy advances, and so forth. The credit agencies or any planned creditor may utilize this data to produce a credit score. How credit scores are determined is definitely not a mystery by any stretch of the imagination.

Credit Score Explained

A credit score measurably analyzes data about you to the credit execution of a base example of individuals with comparable profiles. The higher your credit score, the more probable you are to be a decent credit prospect. The less insecure you are, the better your odds of getting credit at a lower financing cost.

At the point when a potential creditor takes a gander at your credit report, they are making a gander at a story from in any event one of the significant credit authorities: TransUnion, Equifax and Experian. These organizations gather record and payment data on you from your creditors. Creditors may report data to only one, two or every one of the three credit departments.

It's essential to comprehend what is in your credit report on every one of the three agencies in light of the fact that since certain loan specialists report to specific credit authorities, you may even have different credit scores at every one of the three. In addition, loan specialists don't counsel each of the three agencies either. In this manner, you might be declined for credit by loan specialists that demand data from specific agencies and you may be affirmed by others.

Credit Score Components

Various variables are utilized by potential banks to decide your credit score. A few variables have more impact than others. The most significant factors regarding effects on your credit score result are the individuals who have to do with payment conduct, credit conduct and debt circumstance.

Payment history: Many of your debt payments are recorded in your credit history, your bill payments, advance payments, credit card payments, store card payments, and so forth, are totally included. Additionally, in the event that you had wrongdoings like late payments or missed payments, the measure of time it took you to address this circumstance will likewise be thought about your credit score.

Extraordinary debt: This incorporates the sums you owe on your records, the various sorts of files you have and how close your parities are to as far as possible. Overdraft understandings, credit card, adjust, store card charges, credit extensions, and so forth are incorporated inside this classification.

New credit: This is a significant factor that incorporates what number of uses for the loan you've made and how as of late you've made them.

Credit history: Lender likewise see to what extent you've had credit, to what extent accounts have been open, and to what extent it has been since you've utilized each record.

A brilliant method to improve your credit score is to take care of the entirety of your tabs on schedule, unfailingly! It's the least expensive, quickest and most productive weapon against terrible credit!

Debt to Credit Ratios

When working with people on credit issues and dealing with the complexities of a credit report score, one notices without question that the debt to credit ratio is important. The debt to credit ratio can have a huge effect on that important home or auto loan or that needed business loan. However when balanced correctly, in accordance with the set standards for good credit from the credit reporting agencies, the debt to credit ratio can provide the much needed improvement for your current credit score.

People are constantly commenting on what a good idea it is to make sure and pay off all of your cards every month in full to make sure to establish good credit and show that one can pay their bills. This is such a misconception and only leads to confusion. Having a revolving balance kept at the right percentage compared to your debt and you are on your way to a better credit report.

Learning about your debt to credit ratio can be one of the important steps to putting yourself in the right frame of mind for credit success. For most Americans the debt to credit ratio is to high and it can be hard to obtain any new offers or loans from banks or financial institutions. For example, you have resolving accounts totaling $10,000 but you currently owe $8,000 which gives you an eighty percent ratio, very high for a buyer of a finance deal to even take a second look at you.

Lenders make the bulk of their money through charging interest, not sending out pretty square cards or annual fees. When looking at any model designed for credit scoring, it likes you to maintain your balances and pay over a length of time and it is driven with your ability to do this, amongst other things.

Being a lender in an institution, if I could see that over a long period of time, you had been able to maintain long-term credit worthiness with a company, it would prompt me to want your business and "interest" as well. As a lender, I know the type of customer that I want to solicit my loans to.

Sub-prime Merchandise Cards can be a great way to balance your debt to credit ratio while still warranting that $350 purchase for that lamp you HAD to have at Macy's. Sub-Prime Merchandise Cards are simply cards carrying a line of credit to buy merchandise from a specific merchant which in most cases turns out to be the company who originally sold you the card.

Some marketers, perhaps due to their obvious benefits to the consumer, have started to market these cards while misrepresenting and misunderstanding how they work in their advertising campaigns. Sub Prime Merchandise Cards report to one or more of the three credit reporting agencies and can help to even out your percentages quickly when it comes to debt to credit ratio.

Do It Yourself Credit Score Repair

You can find Ads everywhere for systems, books and secrets to help fix your credit report score in a hurry with virtually no effort. Many of these programs are featured on TV, in magazines and through Pop up ads online. Some of these marketing ads include claims such as the Tabloids use to promote their unbelievable magazines. Claims such as, "Your credit score can jump 200 points in only 3 hours" or "Create a completely new credit file and fix your credit in only a day". The truth is that there is not any credit program that can guarantee results that fast and no quick fix home remedy that will immediately solve all of your problems.

However, with only a little investment of time and effort, you can produce amazing results and raise your own credit score by yourself, without having to pay some credit repair agency tons of money in order to help. Even the Federal Trade Commission has stated right on their website that anything a credit reporting agency can do for you, you can do for yourself. All that is required is making sure to educate yourself properly with the right books and apply some simple techniques to take the time to Do It Right the first time and produce a better credit score.

There are only a few available books that can really help the average consumer to fix their own credit score and these books are well worth the small price. In order to fix your own credit, you need to know not only credit basics, but also the insider tips and techniques that the credit repair agencies use to fix your credit for you. These are easily applied once you are shown how to do it through the right book and using the right letter templates and time-tested methods.

The Credit Secrets Bible is the most highly recognized reading and program in the online search category when I searched for credit help. The publication, first produced in 1994 and with a new edition out by popular demand this year helps people with insider techniques and tips that the credit bureaus don't want you to know.

Credit report can be easy, can save you thousands of dollars and you can do it yourself and make sure to put yourself on a better road to financial freedom. Find out for yourself how simple it can be and read about more of these insider tips to get you started on your credit score education and a better financial future.

Chapter Two

Credit Scoring and Your Financial History

Your credit history affects your ability to borrow and even creeps up to attack how much money it costs you to borrow once you find yourself actually approved for something. Every creditor, lender or individual interested in someone as a prospective customer has a credit scoring system in place to use with the information you provide when submitting your application. An individual's credit report is essential to anyone out there seeking credit and is very important to any loan officer.

Many thinks of credit scoring systems as very vague "Wizard of Oz" type all powerful machines which control your number at a high speed. These credit scores are based on a statistical system however and are as easy to explain as the mystical "wizard". The systems that were created to calculate your credit score use real world data and enable the lender or creditor to view the individual objectively.

Some of these include the number and the different types of bank accounts an individual has, outstanding debts, history of bill paying, debt to credit ratios, any collections accounts that have been brought against the individual, bankruptcies and other factors determined more by the individual and his or her financial portfolio.

By comparing the history and background of one individual against the background of thousands of other consumers with financial situations and payrates that are similar, one can better predict the outcome of a loan offer made to this individual. It is easier to predict future habits based on the person's ability in their past and see whether it is likely that debt will be managed well and repaid in the agreed upon time.

The mathematical system used by credit scoring systems has proven to lenders that it can be a strong predictor of one's future ability to repay their credit or debt to an individual company. The system created was designed to place more emphasis on history and less emphasis on individual statistics, which are variable.

You can request your credit report through a number of ways but it will not help if you do not have the education and knowledge in order to read it and determine what you can do to raise your own credit score. Make sure to arm yourself with the knowledge through the right book, audio tape or program and you can put your credit report to work for you and be on the path to a better credit score.

Credit Reporting and How Your Credit Score is Determined

There are many people out there who are unaware of what their credit score is or how much it already could be affecting their wallet or could in the future if habits are not changed. Lenders have been using your credit report score in determining whether or not to grant you a loan and to calculate your interest rate for some time now. The loan officer knows what a powerful tool for predicting future behavior the credit score can be and has proved over and over again to be.

Credit scores measure risk through mathematical calculations, using statistical research to view each consumer. FICO, which is the most widely used credit-score formula was created by Fair Isaac. FICO scores are now often requested for such simple applications in categories such as cell phone providers, utility companies, landlords and even prospective employers. It seems that your credit score can affect a lot more than just getting that low interest rate on that all important home or auto loan.

Managing your credit score and knowing your score and what is included on the report should be a priority for anyone. First you need to educate yourself on how your credit score is determined and calculated by these reporting companies.

In order to calculate the score of just one individual, FICO credit system uses 22 pieces of data, which they collect from each of the three major credit bureaus and use in their analysis. The system seems to break down into separate categories and then put together a composite of all category scoring into a final outcome. Payment history, types of credit used, current debt, length of your credit history and new credit are the determining factors in credit scoring.

Even though people may think so, income is not a factor in a credit score and does not reflect upon the final score. Individual or variable factors are not taken account in a credit score so that the final outcome is more mathematical and analytical in nature, not using personal feelings or considering circumstance. Credit scores are simply predictors for future behavior based on past experience and behaviors.

The lowest possible credit score to have is 300 with the highest rating an 850. The higher your score is, the lower the possible risk to a creditor, and the better your interest rates are going to be. Having a score that is 800 or above is hard to obtain, with only an average of between 13-18% of the population having an 800 or higher credit rating. The average median credit score is more on average between 700 and 750.

Your FICO score is different from your credit reports. If you want to take a look at your credit reports, this is ALWAYS the place to start when it comes to credit repair. In 2003, The Fair and Accurate Credit Transaction Act entitles you to a free credit report from each of the three major credit bureaus once a year. Make sure to request yours to keep up to date on what is changing on your report.

Staggering when you request the reports also helps you to keep up to date on any changes and staggering the reports will also help you to spot bad information sooner. Many places can help you to obtain your credit report. A comprehensive list is included below to help you to getting your hands on your credit report.

The most detailed information to be found online when it comes to credit scoring seems to be from the creators themselves. You can go to the Credit Education area for the most up to date information regarding your credit report and rights. They offer all three credit bureau's reports, which is highly recommended.

Because credit reporting is based on time and all three agency do not run like clockwork when it comes to which tasks are at hand. When one bureau reports something and when another bureau dates something could vary greatly. It would be impossible for each bureau to keep track of there reports all on the same schedule.

You will find that each bureau has different schedules and ways of reporting which makes it the most advantageous to have all three reports. You want to be able to make sure that all three bureaus show the same things and that one does not report something that the others do not, which is often the case when one bureau receives a collection activity notice and the others don't.

Build Credit History

You can actually build credit history for yourself it is not hard and you can do it quickly and easily. Basically, you have to supply the credit bureaus with what they want. This is an invaluable credit score secret.

It is worth remembering that it isn't only about getting a mortgage when you need to boost your credit, many people from landlords to potential new employees might be interested in your credit history to test if you are a risky investment. As they can't know the real person immediately they will check the report to get an idea of your character.

Make good practices part of your everyday financial dealings and you will build credit history much quicker than you thought. This is how you start credit repair yourself.

1. Obtain a copy of your credit report.

You can get one free copy of your credit report per year and you should do so and then dispute any negative, out-of-date or inaccurate information that is on it. Most people don't even do this first simple step and their credit report gathers all kinds of negative entries over the years. The fact is that you can easily remove items that don't act in your favour if you dispute them. By not disputing them they will always be there acting against you.

2. Add some good accounts.

Some people overlook this easy step. A couple of checking and savings accounts look good on your report. Any potential lender will see this as a sign of stability and they will look more favorably at lending you money. This is feeding them what they want to see.

Use a maximum of 30% of your credit limit. Apply for a credit card if you don't have one. The conditions attached to the card aren't really important you just have to be responsible with it, that is to say use some of the available credit and regularly pay it off. Again you are showing them what they want to see; discipline.

3. Get a loan.

This is a great way to have a variety of credit on your report. You increase your score by demonstrating you can manage different types of credit. Obtain a small loan from a local bank and pay it off.

So, not all credit repair secrets are really "secrets".

Chapter Three

Build Credit Score Secrets

As you enter adulthood, or even if you are rebounding from a string of bad credit blunders, you'll want to build your credit score in order to make your financial life easy. It probably doesn't sound like a fun or necessary thing to do, but it is. Without credit, or with bad credit, you get denied for a job, have a hard time renting an apartment, and getting approved for a car loan can be difficult. It can also be quite costly, as a person without credit is considered at risk to the lender, so they make you pay a hefty premium and interest rates on your loan.

Steps to Build Credit Score

What you want to do is create a credit file. This does by no means hard or time consuming. You just have to do the things you already do in your everyday life a little different.

The first step is to get a credit card. Even though many people will tell you credit cards are evil, they are a necessary evil. Without using credit, you limit yourself from building a positive credit report. All you need to do is get a credit card, use it minimally, and pay it off in full. Lenders like to see that people have extended credit to you and that you know how to use it responsibly.

That means you not only need a credit card, but you need to keep it active. Do not max out your card, just make one minimal purchase enough so there is some activity. Then pay it off. It can literally be a $0.10 purchase if you like. Just keep it active. This will help build your credit score.

If you have bad credit and cannot get approved for a credit card, try a department store or gas card. These are typically much easier to get approved for, but they also generally come with very high interest rates - so be careful with these.

If you cannot get approved for store card, then get a secured credit card. This is a card that is backed by other assets you may have. For example, to get a $500 secured card, you may have to verify that you have $500 cash and set it aside in case you do not pay off the debt. The purpose here is simply to build credit, so again all you want to do is use it minimally. In three to six months the use of your secured card should help you obtain a major credit card without a problem. At that point, you can cancel the secured card.

Secrets to Building a High Credit Score

The advantages of having a high credit score are many; first of all you will have access to cash on demand. You will be able to walk into any lenders office and walk out with as much money as you like for things like cars, credit cards and home loans. In this book, I will go over the secrets to building a high credit score.

The first step to getting a high credit score is taking care of any negative accounts on your report or accounts that may be about to affect your credit report in a negative way. This will involve taking a good look at your credit report and challenging items such as collection accounts, late payments, charge-offs and other derogatory items.

It is important to know that in terms of the credit score formula, a lot of emphasis is put on accounts that are the most recent this is why you want to stop new negatives from appearing on your reports. You might have to settle with collection agencies or get caught up with past due bills to stop the damaging effect they will have on your credit scores.

Once this has been taken care of, the secret to building up your score to a high number would be to create a long history of timely payments on your credit reports. A high credit score means that you were able to take out credit accounts time and time again and pay off the balance without missing payments or defaulting on the loan.

The only way to do this is by keeping accounts in good standing for a period of time. It does require some effort but well worth the effort in the long run.

Easy Steps to a Better Credit Score

Buy a home, drive a nice car, apply for a small business loan -- an impressive credit report bodes well at these turning points in life. The first step to improving your credit is being informed about your financial standing. Once you understand what items are in your credit report you can then work on removing the negative ones. Adding positive items to your credit report is also very important, especially if you have little to no credit history. These few steps should allow you to see an improvement in just 3-6 months. Maintaining good standing in your accounts (both bank and credit cards) will greatly improve your score.

Request Your Report

First things first, where can you go to find out where you stand? There are many sites out there that offer free credit reporting once a year. There are 3 credit reporting agencies that companies use in retrieving your credit report: Experian, Equifax, and TransUnion. Each company's website offers a free trial to show their version of your credit report. Yes, their "version" meaning sometimes one might report something slightly different or not at all. So it is important to check all three versions to ensure accuracy of the information.

It is a common misconception that looking at your own credit report reflects negatively on you and your credit score. This is an absolute fallacy. When you check your own credit report it is known as a "soft credit check" and it is NOT recorded in your credit report nor does it reflect negatively on you in any way. Checking your own credit report is a good thing, and I recommend you do it at least once a year.

Remove Negative Items

There are several factors that could possibly reflect badly on you in your credit report. The most well-known negative element is bankruptcy. Bankruptcy will stay on your credit report for 7-10 years. Avoid filing for bankruptcy at all costs.

The easiest way to do this is to be financially responsible. Don't apply for loans you might not be able to pay back on time and do not charge anything to your credit cards if you don't have the cash on hand to pay more than the minimum monthly payment. Divorce also reflects badly on your credit report.

One of the easier things to remove from your report is a revolving account. Limit yourself to one savings and one checking account each at the same bank. If you have more than 2 or 3 credit cards, then you should strongly consider consolidating your current balances into just a handful of cards. Too many revolving accounts look bad on your credit report, even if they are all in good standing. If you apply for a loan or credit card and you are rejected, do not apply for another one for several months. You are actually less likely to be approved once the rejection appears on your report, and having multiple rejections is very unattractive to others viewing your report. Work on improving your credit and then go back and apply if you still feel the need.

Add More Positive Elements

Now here are some positives that you can add to your credit report. If you currently have little or nothing in your credit history, then I would suggest getting a retail charge card (e.g. an Ox Publishing credit card). One good thing about a retail line of credit is that you cannot use it one a whim. You are only able to use an Ox Publishing charge card to buy books published by them; therefore, you won't use it for an impulse buy, but it is a great way to carefully build your credit. Most popular clothing stores also offer a credit card, but I wouldn't suggest these for most people because clothes are often an impulse buy.

Maintain Good Financial Standing

Monitor your credit report carefully. Each of the aforementioned sites offers constant credit monitoring for a nominal monthly fee. You may also want to check with you banking institution. If your bank offers online banking, they likely also offer credit monitoring.

Top 5 Credit Score Myths

If you've read any number of these articles, you know the high level of importance I place on your credit score and credit score repair. They're like the permanent records your grade school teachers always warned you about come to life. Suddenly, every financial decision you've ever made is under the microscope for lenders and creditors to see should you ever try for a loan.

But there's another side to your credit score - a misunderstood side. Most people don't have the first clue about what exactly goes into their credit score, through no real fault of their own. You can thank the Fair Isaac Corporation for that. They're the company behind the FICO credit scores, the most widely used credit scoring model in the US, and they like to play their cards close to the chest, meaning they don't let consumers or lenders know precisely how they calculate your score.

Since FICO doesn't let anyone in on their secrets, it's up to the lenders and consumers to try and interpret their smoke signals, and that generally leads to confusion. So, in the interest of shining some light on your credit score and clearing up some of the confusion, here are 5 of the top myths about your score:

1. Your credit score is your permanent record. Like I said before, most people equate their credit reports and scores to a report card for adults. And much like a report card and the grades that come with them, a lot of people only think about their scores when they actually see them. If their score is high, all is right with the world. If their score isn't where they thought it would be though, they generally don't feel so hot; some of them even seeing their score as a reflection of themselves.

But here's the thing: just like your grades in school, your credit score can, and usually will change. There isn't really anything permanent about it; it changes every time you look at it. So if you don't like what you see, you can work to change it.

2. Even looking at your score will drive it down. A lot of people who check their credit reports may notice that they have a lot of inquiries on file, especially if they've been shopping for credit in the past few months. While it's true that having too many inquiries on your report can dock you a couple of points per inquiry, those are only the "hard" inquiries - those made by lenders and creditors into your file to determine your financial risk. Anytime you check your credit score yourself, it's labeled as a "soft" inquiry and doesn't ding your credit score.

3. You need a balance to build credit. You gotta spend money to make money. That saying may apply in some cases, but not

to credit. You don't need to maintain a balance to build up your credit. According to FICO, only 35% of your credit score is made up of your payment history, and many creditors aren't looking to see whether or not you carry a balance over each month on your credit cards. Worry about keeping current on your bills rather than what kind of balance you should maintain.

4. When you get married, so do your credit scores. While you do promise to stay with your spouse through richer or poorer, your credit score doesn't. Even though your significant other's credit lines may show up on your credit report, and vice versa, after marriage, the individual credit reports remain as just that - individual. Your account may show up on their report, but it remains in your name - only accounts opened jointly affect both parties.

5. Disputing every negative item on your credit report boosts your score. This is

certainly a myth I'm familiar with. A lot of credit repair companies tell you that the quickest and best way to dispute all negative items on your credit report. If the credit bureaus don't respond within 30 days, the item will be wiped off your report, and your score will raise.

The problem with that is sometimes (usually) those items come back. Not only that, you could also be taken to court for lying about your accounts, and no one wants that. Rather than fall for empty promises, work on resolving any negative accounts legally, and if you need help, consult a credit repair service that can help you achieve your goals without relying on fast tactics.

Raise Your Credit Score in a Flash

You want to buy the latest iPod. Your kid has been begging for a new PlayStation. Your wife has been hinting about a new set of jewelry. You think it's about time to replace your old film camera with the digital one that everybody's using. Your old cellular phone finally gave up on you. The scene is typical. There are so many things you want to buy, there's just one problem: bad credit score. You can't get a credit card from anywhere. If you only knew how to raise credit score, you'd do it in a jiffy.

If you think there is no one who can help you raise credit score, you're absolutely wrong. Yes, you may be tired of those programs crawling all over the Internet that guarantee to raise your credit score but has no results at all, don't fret. There must be something else you haven't tried yet. Credit Secrets Bible is one of those programs that you see on the Internet that helps you with your bad credit. What makes it different from the rest, though, are the things that it teaches you and the truths about the credit system that you never knew.

How can Credit Secrets Bible help you raise credit score? The credit system is actually full of little secrets, and Credit Secrets Bible exposes you to these secrets. Once you know of these secrets, you will get to see how you can use them to your own advantage. You will get to learn how to repair your own credit yourself, the secrets to start getting pre-approved credit cards in you mail box, learn about scams and what can really help you build your credit. How much you charge and how much you pay each month is also relevant, so you also get to learn about that strategy. You get a copy of a short letter that is guarantees you will never get a call from those collection agencies. You will learn about the "4th largest Credit Bureau" and learn why not minding them may cost you thousands. You also get to learn the little trick people have been using to double their credit card limits.

With all that and more, not knowing how to raise credit score will be a thing of the past. Raise your credit and get your credit cards approved. Go ahead and start building your credit -- because you deserve the finer things in life.

Chapter Four

Repairing Your Credit Score

You know how important is your credit score for the balance of your financial life. Keeping your credit score high will ensure that the interest rates you pay will remain low. It will also make you eligible for all kinds of loans and credit cards. Everyone pays attention to your credit score, your bank, your employer, your landlord, your cell phone company, everybody. Here are some tips to keep your credit score high and balanced.

Ask for a higher credit card limit

Here's a tip to keep your credit card balance low. The amount of money you owe as a percentage of your total credit limit counts a lot to your credit score. For example if you have a $5000 credit limit and your credit card balance is $2500 you are at the 50% level, which is relatively high. What you can do to reduce your balance-level is to ask for a higher credit limit. For example if you are approved for a $10000 credit limit and you still owe $2500, you will automatically move to a 25% balance-level.

Know your credit score status

Find a way to order your credit reports from the credit bureaus, especially if you are not approved for a loan or for a credit limit raise. It is highly likely that there are errors on these reports. These errors are caused by lack of verification of information the credit bureaus receive from the creditors. Take a good look at the reports and look for these errors. It's up to you to keep your credit report clean so that it will reflect your financial status. You can then write a letter to the credit bureau asking them to correct the errors. Supply any information or documents as proofs.

Build a strong credit history

As time goes by you are building what the experts like to call Credit-History. Your history has a great impact on your credit score. If you have a long history and a positive financial behaviour, then everybody will be more confident and will lend you their money. Therefore it wouldn't be wise to cancel that old credit cards you don't use because you found a better deal somewhere else. The accounts associated with old credit cards remain active and there's a positive credit-history already created for you. Why not use those cards every once in a while to keep the accounts running?

Don't be fooled by credit repair companies

The best way to repair your credit score is to do it yourself. If you don't know what to do and you are ready to trust one of the thousands of credit repair companies out there, then you better think twice. More than half of them are a scam. It seems that everyone and their brother establishes such a company. It's difficult to discover the legitimate ones. Never pay such a company before they provide their services. Always ask information about your legal rights and be aware not to be involved in any illegal activities without even know it.

Make arrangements with the creditors

Sometimes it's a good idea to talk to your lender about that last late payment. Ask them if it's possible to erase it from your credit history. Some goodwill will never hurt you and you'll have the chance to develop a relationship that could be so beneficial for you in the future. If you don't want to talk to the creditor you can write them a letter and express your request in a polite manner. Remember you've got nothing to lose.

How to Improve Your Credit Score Fast With These Secrets!

First of all to understand how to improve your credit score fast or raise your credit score, it's important to know what areas to concentrate on to give you the best results in the shortest possible time.

It's important to have a good credit score for many reasons. Often people don't realize that a score just a few points higher can save hundreds, even thousands of dollars when they apply for and get a home mortgage, for example. If you have a FICO score around 640-660 and you can raise it to a very good score of 760-780, and you take out a 30-year term home mortgage, you would save about $3000 per year. That adds up to $90,000 savings on that same mortgage!

And raising your score may not be that hard for you to do. Going over the following tips and some secrets you may find a few you can apply immediately and see fairly fast results. Even just a few points can make a difference in your borrowing ability and show you how to improve your credit score fast.

1. About 30-35% of your payment history is reflected in your FICO credit score. No matter what happens, make sure to make payments on time. I make mine 4-5 days early online. Making your payment online is important. You know it's not going to get lost in the mail. Also I make the payment early because websites may have technical problems. If you waited to the last minute you may not be able to get into the website. And I think it looks better to the credit card company if you pay a little early.

If you know you'll have enough money in your checking account you can set up automatic payments also. This is good if you foresee any problems with possible emergencies where you might have to go out of town or hospitalizations coming up, etc.

2. About 30% of your credit score is based on how much you owe. If possible try to keep your balances on your credit cards to less than 50% of the limit on each card. The more below 50% the better.

3. Most people don't know that 15% of your FICO score is based on your credit history. So if you have a credit card that is not being used with a zero balance, and have no activity, it can lower your score. So charge something small each month and pay it off so you build up your credit history.

4. New credit. Make sure not to open up any new accounts. 10% of your FICO credit score is based on how many new accounts you open. This also applies to auto or car loan shopping. If you're shopping rates at several companies, do it in a short period of time - within two weeks. Don't drag it out. Making several

requests could affect your FICO credit score. It may be better to just get the loan through your credit union rather than have the finance officer at the car dealer shop around. Each inquiry he/she makes is reflected with inquiry marks on your credit report.

5. 10% of your FICO credit score is based on your mix of loans. You probably can't do much to change this except - if you don't have a credit card, get one,

6. Last but not least, if you don't have a credit report, obtain or get a free copy from each of the three major credit-reporting agencies, Equifax, TransUnion and Experian. Go over each carefully and write a letter with documentation if you find any mistakes that are not in your favor.

These are a few of the best ways to show you how to improve your credit score or raise your credit score fast! It really doesn't take that long to raise it a few points and it can make a big difference in your borrowing ability. There are a lot more secrets and trade secrets not included in this short article. With a little more research you can find solutions and repair your credit too.

Surefire Ways to Repair a Bad Credit Score

There are a number of reasons why you may find yourself in a bad credit situation. But whatever the reason for your bad credit, you must find a way to repair a bad credit score. Increasing your credit score and eliminating bad credit records will give you more benefits and freedom.

Here are some tips on how to repair a bad credit score:

Pay on or before due dates. If you want to repair a bad credit score, avoid missed and late payments. A negative record can hurt your credit record and is not a good thing in raising your credit score. Paying on time will add positive records on your credit history and increase your credit score.

Always know your credit limit and your balance. To repair a bad credit score, you should be cautious about your credit limit and balance. Be sure that your credit card company reports this information accurately. Do not go over your credit limit to avoid decrease on your credit score. It is much better if you can afford to pay more than your minimum payment. Keeping your credit balance around 30% of your credit limit will help you raise your credit score.

Always check your credit report for inaccuracies. Detect and dispute any errors as early as possible and contact your creditors to make the necessary correction.

Live within your means. Your goal is to repair a bad credit score, so try to re-structure your spending habits. Live within your means and avoid unnecessary expenses. Make a finance plan around your means and pay your debts on time to build a good credit history.

Read books or seek credit counseling to repair a bad credit score. If you are suffering from a poor credit rating, credit counseling can help you bargain a lower interest rate and improve your credit score.

Credit Score Rating System

Understanding the credit score rating system is of the essence for anyone who uses or wishes to establish or restore credit. And you don't have to know all the intricacies that go into calculating your score; just the basics will do.

The basics of the credit scoring system are not that difficult to understand. This information used to be a closely guarded secret until an act of congress forced Fair Isaac, the creator of the most used credit scoring model, to disclose it. Previously, consumers were forced to fly in the dark, as it were, on something that has such a great impact on their lives.

Defined in simple terms, your credit score is a three digit number that indicates your creditworthiness. Needless to say, a lower score indicates bad risk and a high score indicates good risk.

The patriarch of credit scores is the FICO score as it is the one that most creditors use. And though you typically will get this score when you apply for credit, not all credit bureaus supply it directly to consumers. Only two companies can supply you the real FICO credit score.

The FICO score was created by Fair Isaac Corporation and as you might have guessed, the name FICO is actually an acronym of its creator. It is a number between 300 and 850.

There are pretty few people on either extreme of the score. Most people fall somewhere in between. And it is okay to attempt to attain the perfect score, 850, but it is not all that important and could cause you unnecessary stress. What really matters is the range you are in.

A score of between 720 and the maximum 850 used to be considered prime. But after the mortgage meltdown that started somewhere in 2007 and the ensuing credit crisis the bar was raised. You now need a score of at least 740 to 750 (depending on who's looking) to be considered for the best interest rates in loans, credit cards and other forms of credit.

How is your credit score calculated?

Most of the details of the credit score rating system are still closely guarded secrets. But the basics, which suffice for the average consumer, are as follows:

Your payment history accounts for 35% of your score: A good payment history over a lengthy period of time is what counts here.

You debt to credit ratio accounts for 30%: Maxing out on your revolving credit (such as credit cards) is not a good thing. Fair Isaac considers what you owe on each account as well as in total.

Length of your credit history (15%): The longer your history, the better. This is the reason you should start building credit as early as possible, even after a bankruptcy.

Variety of accounts (10%): A "healthy mix" of types of credit is desired. Also, riskier types of credit such as credit cards often score lower than mortgages, car and school loans.

Number and of accounts (10%): Too few credit accounts can hurt your score as can too many. Applying for new credit frequently can hurt your FICO credit score as it indicates risk (you appear desperate).

You should also be aware that your credit rating will differ with each bureau. This is mainly because different creditors report to different bureaus and therefore each bureau's data can differ from one of or both the twos'.

As if to add more confusion to the whole credit score rating system, each major credit reporting bureau refers its score by a different name. Equifax calls theirs the

BEACON score, Transunion calls it the FICO Risk Score and Experian calls it FICO II.

You are not done with the credit score-naming mumbo jumbo just yet. FICO also created what is known as the FICO Expansion Score. This was created for people with scanty history such as recent immigrants. This score considers nontraditional credit data such as utility information and public records.

Think you're done? There is the Vantage score and Next Gen score and more (plus more coming as the credit reporting system continues to evolve).

To avoid the confusion about the credit score ratings system, just go for the score that most creditors use, which is the FICO score. It is worth to repeat that only two entities supply this score directly to the consumers and not all the credit reporting bureaus do. Also, your score does not come free and if it does it is with other strings attached.

Chapter Five

Benefits of Good Credit

Proper credit will allow you to do many things from getting a mortgage or a vehicle, to getting into post-secondary education, getting a great job, or opening your own business. Just as you feel better about lending money to a friend who paid you back quickly the first time, and creditors will be more willing to lend you money when you have a good credit rating. If you are looking to get a loan, having good credit can definitely work in your favor as many lenders will give a better interest rate to people with good credit. With good credit you can also earn rewards points on credit cards that can be redeemed for different things, depending on the card like cash or credit towards a trip. Another benefit to having good credit is credit card companies will offer you higher credit limits. It is not unheard of for some people with good credit to have upwards of $25,000 in available credit on their cards. Of course, you have to be careful with such a high credit limit, you definitely don't want to use the credit if you don't have the funds to cover it or you will be paying hundreds in interest.

If you have already tainted your credit rating, it's still possible to get back to having a great credit rating. It will take time of course, but it's definitely worth doing so you can enjoy all the benefits that having good credit brings. The temptation to borrow money is everywhere, so it takes willpower to say no, but the less credit you have available the less you will use.

If you are in financial trouble and want to get back your good credit rating, there are companies that are ready and willing to help you. Many of these companies are good, sound financial companies, but some are there to take advantage of those seeking help with their debt. It is important to research the company before you sign up for a debt solution company. Go online and check the reviews of the company before you sign up.

Once you find a good, reputable debt settlement company, all you have to do is give them a call and see what they can do for you. They should offer debt settlement, which means that they will work with your creditors to settle your debt; in many cases, for only 40-60 percent of what you owe, because when your creditors know you are in financial trouble they will be more lenient because they don't want you to file bankruptcy. If you do, they will not get paid, so they would rather get some money than none. Find a clear debt solution to help give you an affordable monthly payment that fits your budget, which will get you back on the right track.

Is Good Credit Really Worth the Effort?

Individuals struggle daily to meet their financial obligations, avoiding bad credit by paying their bills on time and working and putting off pleasures to pay interest on excessive debt to achieve good credit. The struggle is truly difficult at times to avoid bankruptcy or home foreclosure, but is good credit really worth the effort? The following article will endeavor to answer this difficult question, and might surprise you.

The real estate bust has left countless households paying off home mortgages that far exceed what they could sell their homes for in the current market, and many others find themselves burdened by high interest credit card debt and are drowning in financing payments with little end in sight. Is good credit really worth it and at what point do the benefits not outweigh the struggles.

Faced with an upside down real estate market many are making the difficult decision to walk away from their homes, downsize and let the banks foreclose. Bankruptcy, foreclosure, and the resulting bad credit is becoming more enticing than the negatives. Frustrated and upside down, consumers are beginning to ask what were the benefits of their hard earned good credit over the years, as the credit crisis dried up many lending avenues regardless of your credit score.

Your credit amounts to your financial reputation, and there are certainly ethical concerns about walking away from your freely accepted obligations. Loans and credit cards are often accepted willingly, not taking into consideration a possible turn of fortune or unforeseen events. The benefits of good credit include better financing terms, lower rates, easier payoff schedules and approvals for otherwise difficult loans. These benefits can be quite compelling and can make the costs of financing in your life much more manageable.

In current times though, many have found themselves weighing the loss of their good credit benefits with the gains in achieving debt relief from their current herculean debt struggles. If you are overburdened, and your current debt burden seems hopeless, one should not rule out bankruptcy and debt relief solutions that are designed to help. Bad credit and the loss of good credit benefits will result, for a time, but in some circumstances this can still be a sound financial decision.

A struggle to maintain good credit is noble, without doubt, but financial missteps are a part of life. I only recommend you look closely at your situation and do not rule out the possibilities that are available. Bad credit is not the end of the world, and can be improved over time, and everyone deserves a second chance in my opinion.

Everyone's financial situation is unique, and cash flow problems can vary, but a sober assessment of your situation is never harmful and sometimes a fresh start is just what is needed.

Maintaining Good Credit After Bankruptcy

How to maintain positive credit can seem like an impossible task to many people plagued by bad credit and debt history. For them the question of whether it is even possible seems tantamount to how to actually do it. Good credit however is nothing difficult, far from being impossible. When understood clearly, credit in itself is no mystery and therefore tackling it is no mystery either. The benefits of good credit are endless and like any self-sustained cycle, having good credit leads to better credit in the future, which is easier to pay off and thereby helps maintain a positive credit.

In order to understand how to maintain positive credit, it helps to know what causes bad credit in the first place. Factors such as tardiness contribute towards giving a poor impression of your finances and will contribute towards a negative credit. When bills are paid late, or not paid at all, it is likely to appear on your financial records. Furthermore, when debts are extended for long periods of time, or accrued to unreasonable extents, they also cause a negative impact. The answer is therefore simple. Paying all your bills on time, well before the due time if possible, and keeping your debt low is the key to maintaining positive credit.

Once you are sure that you are paying all your bills on time, work on paying off any existing debt you may have. It goes without saying that you should limit future debt until all history of debt has been cleared or is well on its way to being cleared. This will help you get better credit, and then any loans or savings you try to get in the future, you will have easier interest rates on them, which will make it more manageable for you. Keeping your debts and bills in check, you should move your focus onto your finance records in general.

Carefully manage and assess all your finances. Even though you cannot see your actual credit score, you can request to see your credit report, which will have a record of all your accounts and finances. Analyze these very carefully for any discrepancies that may exist and be sure to rectify them immediately if you do. If you have many accounts that you do not use, shut them down. There is no need to take on the liability of so many accounts if you are not going to be using them. They only contribute towards a poor credit record.

Finally, make sure you have a well maintained financial and account record. Keep track of all your bills and debt, and work towards paying them off, at a steady and timely rate. Good credit has all the benefits in the world to offer you and bad credit all the harm in the world. Once you know how to maintain positive credit your future finances and decisions should have no reason to suffer, whether you're looking to get a new apartment, a new job, a new home or a new car.

The Advantages of Having a Good Credit Score

There are many advantages and benefits of having and maintaining a good credit score. If you have a credit score of 720, 740, or 760 and up, you have a good score. With high credit scores you will be able to save money each month with lower interest rates on all your financial products.

You will also notice you get a better reception by the car salesmen, home lenders, and even insurance salesmen when you step into their office. They know they have a better chance with closing the sale with you because they can get you approved for a loan at a low rate that you can afford and one that you will be happy with.

A above average credit score will entitle you to demand the best interest rates on home loans, home equity loans, credit cards, car loans, personal loans and more. And in most cases lenders should have no problem accommodating your requests. You've earned your credit now put it to good use.

Another of the advantages of having good credit or good scores to be more precise since you do have to maintain a good score with all 3 of the major credit reporting agencies - Equifax, Experian, and Transunion - is that potential employers will not turn down your application because of your credit history. You stand a better chance of landing a job with a high score as opposed to a low score.

Even if you do not agree with the way most companies use credit scoring information, if you want to get into their game, you have to play by their rules.

And when you do play by their rules, you get to enjoy the benefits of low rate balance transfer offers even when credit is drying up for less than qualified applicants. You still get the perks of being disciplined and not overextending yourself and spending more than you could afford to pay back.

As you can see, there are many benefits and advantages of having a good credit score. To get into the high 700+ credit score range, pay all your bills on time. Stay on top of the due dates like a hawk. Only use a small portion of the balance - less than 25% is ideal. Keep accounts open - 10 to 15 years at a minimum. And don't apply for credit you do not need. Follow these simple steps and you'll be on your way to the best deals on credit anywhere.

Chapter Six

A Good Credit Score Means More Than Just Getting a Loan

When you think of the benefits of having a good credit score, you usually start with how your score affects your ability to get financing. A good score makes it easier to get a loan such as a car loan or mortgage, and it is key in getting a low-interest rate. A bad credit score will make lenders leery of giving you money so even if they are willing to approve your application (something that certainly isn't a sure thing now days), they are going to make you pay more for the loan in the form of higher interest rates to offset the risk that you will default on the loan.

Because of how your credit score gets factored into loans, the simple three digit number that is your score can play a huge role on your overall quality of life. They way it limits or opens up opportunities can determine the size home you are able to purchase, the car you drive, and how much of your earnings go toward assets that increase your overall wealth versus generating profits for the bank (which can affect future big-ticket purchases, your children's education, your retirement, etc.).

But this is not the end of the story. Credit scores which were initially created as a tools lenders could use to quickly determine credit risk, as opposed to digging through each item of your credit reports in an effort to determine your credit worthiness, have been adopted by other industries as well.

Today, not only will your credit score play a role in how your paycheck gets spent, it can affect how much is in your paycheck in the first place. Many employers will use the credit scores of job applicants to aid in the hiring process. Reading through resumes and checking references is a time-consuming process so credit scores are used as a shortcut. Applicants with poor credit scores are viewed as less dependable and trustworthy and will have a harder time even being considered for a position when competing against similarly qualified individuals with good credit. They may not even be given a chance for an interview. Additionally, in certain industries where employees have access to money such as banks, a low credit score automatically disqualifies a person from working there.

Car insurance companies are another group that have adopted the use of credit scores to help determine risk. Studies have shown that drivers with low credit scores are more likely to file insurance claims. And since claims cost the insurance companies money, they want to make sure that the people more apt to file them are charged accordingly. For this reason, the vast majority of auto insurance companies factor in your score when drawing up a policy. The lower your score is, the more you will have to pay in insurance premiums.

Credit card companies also take your credit score into account, which is something most people were aware of, but not everyone realizes the extent of it. Since a credit card is similar to a loan in that you are granted a line of credit that you are required to pay back with interest, it makes sense that credit card companies factor your score into how much credit you can get approved for and at what interest rate. What not everybody realizes is that these figures are not fixed. A credit card companies like to include a "universal default" provision in their contracts in which they reserve the right to monitor your credit reports and increase the credit card interest rate if you have late payments or other negative items added to your credit reports, even if they are completely unrelated to the credit card account. Since credit card debt is unsecured and can be dismissed in a bankruptcy, credit card companies work hard to make sure that if your finances get out of control, they are going to collect as much money from you as possible. Any indication that you might be having trouble making payments and they may start working to offset any future losses.

As you can see, a good credit score opens up a world of opportunities and has benefits many people didn't even realize were there. On the flip side, a bad credit score can be a huge roadblock causing people to have to work much harder in just about every facet of their finances.

Why Bad Credit Lenders Will Need to Adjust What is Considered Good Credit

As a report on your financial reputation your credit score is used by countless bad credit lenders to determine approval for various instruments ranging from loans to credit cards. With the recent credit implosion, economic downturn, and real estate market bust the bad credit lenders will be forced to adjust what is considered a good credit score for approval, helping consumers get approved.

Your consumer credit score is simply an assessment of your reported financial history and your credit is a subjective number used by lenders to determine your credit worthiness. The unintended consequence of the credit and economic implosion is a statistically increasing number of American households with negative marks on their credit reports. Foreclosures, bankruptcies, late payments due to job loss or crushing debt has left many good credit holders suddenly finding themselves with bad credit status.

So how will this affect the market, and what behavior can we expect from lenders in the future? The good news is this ultimately will benefit the consumer. As credit availability increases and the economy turns, lenders will again be in a situation of high competition for potential borrowers. When the tide has turned these lenders will be forced to assess the credit worthiness of their bad credit applicants and will find themselves with a much smaller pool of good credit applicants to lend to. This will force adjustments on the good credit lenders to meet their demands for customers to lend money to as well as the bad credit lenders.

Reversely, credit will become more important than ever. With lower standards because of less availability of good credit borrowers, lenders, as is customary will begin offering more benefits and better terms to the few remaining low risk good credit borrowers. This will lead to lower interest rates, incentive programs, better payoff periods and other perks that can really save you money on your future loans.

So how to best prepare for the direction the loan industry is headed? The wise advice remains the same. Actively work to improve your credit score if you are in a situation to do so, as the benefits make fiscal sense, avoid bad credit decisions if at all possible, and don't beat yourself up if you have had some financial missteps lately, you are not alone. As personal finance times go, this is a time to pick yourself up, dust yourself off, and move forward.

How One Good Credit Consultation Can Save a Life

People are not born with a manual on how to manage credit. As they grew up without good financial education, they often end up in deep credit debt and get scarred for life. A good credit consultation benefits those who want to get out of consumer debt crisis and come up with a rehabilitation plan on how to manage money better.

The proper procedure will not be to jump right away at recommendations for a debt management plan. It is important to trace the milestones that led to the catastrophic personal financial crisis and how the same occurrence can be prevented from happening again in the future. If this is not addressed properly, a vicious cycle of credit crisis might ensue.

A typical output of credit counseling is a sound debt management plan and budget.

Both outputs aim to free the individual from credit and get his finances back on track. The immediate debt relief procedure commonly starts with the consolidation of all debts by the individual, negotiation with all creditors for a lower staggered installment payment which the credit counseling agency distributes to a pool of creditors, and a negotiation for a lower interest rate.

Usually banks and other financial lending institutions extend a lower interest rate for those persons who are under a debt management plan. In this case, people who avail of good credit consultation benefit more from the program if they act on their financial crisis before interest and other charges pile up.

There are credit counseling agencies that specialize in this area of personal finance management. In fact, credit counseling has become a separate and distinct industry altogether. There are agencies specially created for profit and there are also non-profit credit counselors that do the job just as effectively. As defaulting debtors steer away from banks during financial crisis, a good credit counseling agency brings the defaulters into a better understanding with the banking and financial concessions without having them get into a direct and heavy negotiation with these banks.

However, according to the statistics of the National Foundation for Credit Counseling, only about a third of those who undergo a debt management plan becomes rehabilitated and is able to stand on his own afterward. The large portion belongs to those who are beyond financial recovery due to a very low income source or simply a lack of financial discipline.

As they say, prevention is better than cure. But if it is inevitable to be under some sort of credit management assistance, make an appointment for a credit consultation with a reputable credit counseling agency. It pays to be an agency one that will save one from drowning instead of plunging deeper into debt. If before, shopping has brought one into a financial crisis, this time shopping for the best credit counselor is highly recommended.

Mistakes To Avoid To Maintain Good Credit Score

Achieving a favorable credit score can take some time for many people, particularly those facing debts. As such, it is wise to maintain it for the long term to enable you to avail of the benefits that go with having a good score.

Being responsible for one's actions is a must especially when it comes to handling your finances. Remember that it's never a pleasant experience to be in debt, to face foreclosure and worse, to go bankrupt. Note that being in these situations can badly impact your life for up to seven years.

So what other mistakes you need to avoid to ensure that you keep your score moving forward. Experts pointed out several small issues that can also affect your score and even lower it into a mediocre number.

Firstly, don't develop the habit of opening too many credit card accounts. The reason is that every application will reflect on your credit report and will elicit a hard inquiry from the agencies. It's true that offers of cash back, rewards points, sign-on bonuses and zero percent interest on new balance transfers can be quite tempting to accept but control yourself and maintain only one or two accounts as much as possible.

Not paying your credit card bill even for just one month is another issue. Did you know that missing a single payment can cause your score to plunge by 100 points? That's right. But then again, you can recover your good standing in about a year's time as long as you pay promptly every month moving forward. This applies for those who have maintained a good credit score. However, those already facing problems before missing out on a payment can expect to recover in more than a year's time.

Closing an account is also not a good idea. Think many times before deciding on closing your old account as this can have an impact on your score.

Some credit card owners are also in the habit of spending up to their limit. But take heed because this is not a good attitude. This will impact your credit utilization ratio and cause it to soar. If ever you do this, though, you have to find a way to pay your balance off so you can still enjoy using the card.

Being in the know about the date your statement closes is also important. But be careful about gaining additional bill before your statement date as this can be reported and affect your score. What you should do then is to try to maintain a low balance before the agency makes a report. If you can, it would be a good idea to pay off your purchases not long after your make them.

You might also want to check your credit report as often as possible. The Fair Credit Reporting Act now makes it possible to get a free yearly credit report. This is essential so you can check for inaccuracies and other errors in your accounts and balances. MainStreet has revealed that 30 to 40 percent of all credit reports have some error with some already hard to correct or remove.

Ways That a Good Credit Repair Service Can Help Your Situation

The fact that you have thought of asking this question before jumping on the bandwagon and trying to get your credit repair is a very good sign. This means you that you have finally started thinking in terms of value for money. There is no fun in spending a lot of money very quickly.

The smart option is to get value worth two dollars for every single dollar you spend. Hence, before you think of employing a good credit repair service provider, just ask yourself - how exactly well I benefit?

From the intangible point of view, the fact that you have a person to whom you can discuss, analyze and reason as far as your credit repair is concerned will be a huge psychological boost. The fact that the person knows more about credit repair and a lot more about financial management than you do will also be an added advantage.

There is a huge difference in discussing these tactics and strategies with your wife and discussing it with a professional who does this on a daily basis for hundreds of customers.

From the tangible and practical point of view, you can get bad credit removed in a jiffy. That is right. There are numerous instances where individuals are suffering from a low score primarily because they have not remove the negative points stated in the credit report.

Once this defect is removed, the credit report automatically witness is arise. Further, a good credit repair service can help you convince the creditor to send this information on to each and every person to whom you have applied for a loan or a job in the past six months.

There are numerous instances where credit bureaus and lenders are try to work together to keep you in the low credit score. The basic idea is to convert you in to sub prime borrower so that high interest can be charged. In such a scenario, good credit repair service can be a huge asset by your side.

You just have to get the bad credit removed by using all the various the strategies and techniques available in the market. Another significant factor is that the credit repair expert will be aware of all the laws and the latest changes that have been made in your favor or against your favor.

All this will help you plan your finances better in the future. If you try to get bad credit removed with the help of an expert, you shall never fail.

Chapter Seven

How to Rebuild a Good Credit History

Having a good credit history is a good thing that everybody will yearn to have, and given the benefits that come with a good history, it is no doubt why many people are rushing to clean up their reports. It is without doubt that one will have easy access to loans and other forms of credit provided the history on one's file shows a good report. But there are some things that are needed to get it right.

First, you need to ensure that you have no negative information on your file. Negative information such as collections, late pays, charge-offs, inquiries, court judgments and other negative entries sends your score down and affects your rating negatively - this is part of what makes up your history. Thus it becomes imperative that you try to get rid of information that will help in boosting your present score and put your history in a good perspective.

But that's not all. You need to take measures to control the everyday active part of your personal finances too. For instance, you may discover that having 4 or 5 credit cards has actually been hurtful to your file rather than beneficial. You might consider cutting some of these cards to improve your rating. But when you're to do this, ensure you keep old credit accounts open and active as the older they are, the better.

Besides this, you should also reduce expenses you make on your credit accounts to between 20 to 40 percent of the total. It is advised you keep your expenses below 20percent for best and rapid results as it will boost your score significantly.

You should also avail yourself of the opportunity to rebuild a good history and rating by signing up with a competent credit repair agency. An alternative method, if you want more control, is to obtain a restoration-kit and do-it-yourself.

Rebuild & Keep Good Credit Ratings by Understanding Your Credit Cards

Secured Credit Card is similar to a prepaid credit card since the funds you are using are actually yours and not the issuer of the credit card. Generally people who apply for secured credit card or prepaid credit card are people with poor credit or unemployed. Prepaid Credit Card spending limit is the amount of money you loaded to the card. There are no interest or finance charges on a prepaid card. With secured credit card, your credit line could be from 50% to 100% of your deposit depending on the institution giving you the secured credit. Therefore the company giving you the secured credit card has zero risk.

Secured credit card can be very beneficial because it gives you an opportunity to rebuild your credit history and you are able to make purchases just as if you had an unsecured credit card. Many companies require that you have a credit card to make purchases, such as car rental, airline tickets, etc. Ensure that the company issuing the secured credit, routinely reports customers' payment history to any of the three main credit bureaus namely Experian, Equifax and Trans Union. This reporting to the credit bureaus will rebuild your credit history over time.

Closing unnecessary accounts and consolidating your bills to make payments more manageable could be an advantage financially. By not applying for too much credit within a short period of time is another factor that will help in rebuilding your credit rating. Additionally, even though secured credit is like prepaid cards, they do have certain fees attached.

Benefits are similar to that of an unsecured credit card, such as usually being paid interest on your balance in the bank, using Automated Teller Machines

(ATM) to make deposits, withdrawals, and making purchases at participating merchants. Following the above steps will strengthen your credit rating.

Unsecured Credit Cards are issued to individuals with good to excellent credit rating. Credit ratings depend on certain criteria, such as one's ability to repay loans. These criteria include payment history, employment history, and financial stability. Individuals with excellent credit will most likely receive a lower interest rate. A major factor in maintaining excellent credit is making your loan payments on time thus avoiding late fee penalties.

Customers should read the credit agreement to ensure that they understand their obligation to the creditor. Making payments on time will strengthen your credit rating. Unsecured credit cards has numerous advantages such as low interest rates, high credit limit, business name options, no annual fees, and low APRs on balance transfers up to 12 months. Closing unnecessary accounts and consolidating your bills to make payments more manageable could be an advantage financially. By not applying for too much credit within a short period of time is another factor that will help in maintaining a good credit rating.

Rebuilding your credit takes time, patience, and consistency. If you consistently pay your bills on time, you will see an improvement in your credit ratings over time. There are no quick fixes for improving your credit report except for mistakes or inaccuracies that can be corrected, hopefully in your favor. Your credit information is maintained by the credit bureaus namely Experience, Equifax, and Trans Union for seven years. Therefore poor credit information will remain on your report for seven years. The good thing is that as negative information disappears with positive information, this will definitely rebuild your credit rating.

Applying for secured credit card can be very beneficial because it gives you an opportunity to rebuild your credit history, and you are able to make purchases just as if you had an unsecured credit card. Many companies require that you have a credit card to make purchases, such as car rental, airline tickets, etc. Ensure that the company issuing the secured credit, routinely reports customers' payment history to any of the three main credit bureaus namely Experience, Equifax and Trans Union. This reporting to the credit bureaus will rebuild your credit history over time.

Business Credit Card

Business credit cards are very popular for small business owners because of the many benefits they offer. Benefits includes 0% Intro APR on balance transfers, no annual fees, high credit limit, low interest rates, cash rewards, bonus miles, free online account management to choosing card design etc., At iCreditOnline.com we have some of the best business credit cards from American Express, Advantage, Chase, Bank One, Bank of America, Discover, Citibank, Household Bank and more, with online credit card approval. Why waste time going to a bank when you can get a decision in less than 60 seconds with secure online credit card application. Online Credit Card Approval with Online Credit Card Application is fast and easy!

Student Credit Card

Having a student credit card while still living at home or attending school away from home can be an advantage. It gives the student the opportunity to establish credit at an early age and to start asserting their independence. It comes in handy in case of emergency, it is less trouble and safer to carry a student credit card than to carry cash. Parents find student credit cards to be very convenient. They are able to make deposits to their children's account while they are away from home. Students should be careful with their credit card receipts to avoid identity thief.

If you consistently pay your bills on time, obtaining students credit cards is a good way to established credit rating and start building a good credit history while in school. Establishing and maintaining a good credit rating will make it easy to purchase a car, a home or obtaining a personal loan in the future. For students who are not committed to their financial obligation, getting a student credit card is not a good idea. Running up balances, finding yourself in debt, unable to make monthly payments will destroy your credit rating.

Student's credit cards generally have high interest rates. At iCreditOnline.com we offer some of the best student credit cards from Chase and Discover with 0% APR introductory rate for 6 months, no annual fees and online account access. Online credit card approval with online credit card application is fast and easy!

Explanation of some of the credit cards we offer:

0% Intro APR Credit Card or Balance Transfer Credit Card gives you the benefit of using this credit card without making any interest payment on the principal for a stated period of time. This credit card is marketed to individuals with good credit rating who want to transfer balance from a high interest credit card to a 0% intro APR credit card.

Cash Rewards or Cash Back Credit Card earns a percentage on purchases made. This reward or cash back is credited to your account.

Debit Card takes the place of carrying a checkbook or cash. This card is used like a credit card with certain limitations, such as not being able to rent a car. Purchase transactions are contingent upon having enough funds in your checking or savings account to cover the purchase. Verification of funds requires entering your Personal Identification Number (PIN) at a point-of-sale terminal.

Low interest credit card saves you money. Having a good credit rating qualifies you for some of the best low APR credit card offers.

Prepaid Credit Card spending limit is the amount of money you loaded to the card. There are no interest or finance charges on a prepaid card. Therefore the company giving you the prepaid credit card has zero risk. Generally people who apply for prepaid credit card are people with poor credit or unemployed.

Secured Credit Card is secured by the amount of funds you have in your account. Your credit line could be from 50% to 100% of your deposit depending on the institution giving you the secured credit.

Unsecured Credit Card is issued to individuals with good to excellent credit rating. Credit ratings depend on certain criteria, such as one's ability to repay loans. These criteria include payment history, employment history, and financial stability. Individuals with excellent credit will most likely receive a lower interest rate and can receive instant online credit card approval. A major factor in maintaining excellent credit is making your loan payments on time thus avoiding late fee penalties.

Travel Rewards Credit Card benefits may include travel accident insurance, free rental car collision/loss damage insurance, rebate on gasoline purchases, frequent flyer points or bonus miles towards airline flights, free quarterly and annual account summaries.

How to Qualify For and Establish Good Credit

The credit score shows someone how desirable they are to a lender. When a lender sizes you up to determine how much credit, if any to grant you, it usually looking at your credit report and measures your past credit history performance based on your credit score. Generally, a lender usually looks at these 3 keys areas: character, capacity and capital (sometime known as 3Cs) to project how responsibly you handle your credit obligations. Hence, to qualify for and establish good credit, you need to get good score in these 3 areas. Let discuss it one by one.

Character

When you promptly pay principal and interest on your mortgage, student loans, credit card and other loans, you established a good character. By demonstrating a strong sense of character, you persuade the lender to trust that you will make a good-faith effort to pay your bills even if you run into financial difficulties.

Capacity

Capacity measures your financial ability to assume a certain amount of debt. Whenever you apply for a loan, the lender will ask for your annual income statement and your investment portfolio and he/she also want to get to know your other income sources. Many banks set minimum income requirements that your must meet to qualify for certain dollars of credit. The higher your total earning, the larger your credit capacity will be. Besides considering your sources of income, lender also takes into consideration of your existing debts. They prefer it if no more than a maximum of 36 percent of your income pays your total fixed expenses, and if no more that 28 percent of your income pays for housing, either mortgage or rent. The more debt you incur, the less credit lenders extend.

Capital

Lenders consider stocks, bonds, mutual funds, real estate, collectibles, cars and other asset as your capital that they can disposal to retire your debts if your character and capacity do not prove sufficient. Sometimes, lender may need you to pledge your capital/asset for your loan if your character and capacity are not sufficient to persuade lender to approve your application.

The Benefit of Having Good Credit

Lenders love people with good credit record to borrow money from them. That's why people with good credit get a better offer in applying for credit. Among the benefits of being a good credit are: the lower interest rate, faster application approval, more attractive packages with more choices. It's mean "Save More Money If You Have Good Credit". If you have good credit, you even can negotiate with the lender to lower down the interest else you will turn your head to other lender.

In Summary

Having a good credit score means you have more options available to you. You can get loans with better terms and rates and you have more available to you when it comes to types of loans. The credit record build over time, hence it's never too early to start to establish good credit record for yourself and qualify for better options at the time your need it.

Benefits of Improving Credit Report Scores

If you have ever applied for a loan or opened a new account, you have realized just how important your credit score is. This three digit number is what almost everyone uses to determine whether you are a good risk for lending money to or not. Lenders like to see numbers that are above 700. A credit score of 830+ is considered perfect credit.

However, with so much economic upheaval happening, your credit report may be starting to take a hit. There are many benefits of improving credit report scores. Here's a few things to consider.

Know Your Number

You can't fix something if you don't know that it's broken. In order to start working on improving your credit score, you have to know what is there. While you can get a free credit report, it doesn't show you what that all important number is. In order to find out how companies are rating you, you will need to pay a bit extra to get your credit rating number. However, it is well worth the cost. Also, when you are working to improve your credit score, you need to keep a closer eye on things than a once a year inquiry allows.

It's Not Just About Loans

While it's absolutely true that almost no loan can be cleared without checking your credit report, that's not the only thing that can be affected by bad credit. Any place that requires a background check can pull your credit score. This includes your employer and even your landlord if you are trying to rent an apartment. Poor credit suggests a higher chance of irresponsibility and it can really mess up your life.

Know Your Options

There are several things you can do to improve your credit scores. Refinancing is a commonly used strategy. However, make sure you have a solid financial plan or you'll end up right back where you started. You can also take a settlement or file for bankruptcy. Both of these options will reflect poorly on your credit.

However, if the problem is really bad, it may be worth it. Wiping the slate clean can enable you to start over fresh. Either way, make sure that you keep a close eye on your credit so you can assess the impact of each change you make.

Chapter Eight

Enjoy The Benefits Of A Credit Card!!

Do you need a credit card that has to be applied in your name? If so, how do you go about it?

Are you contemplating on getting a credit card? The answer is very simple. It very obviously is a yes. For most people it is quite necessary to get a credit card as it will help them in quite a few ways. Credit cards have of course transformed our lives to a great extent. Revolution is another pattern it can be seen in. Anywhere & everywhere all you find are ads, in newspapers, TVs, shops, websites and every other place you go to asking you to apply for one. If you take a closer look you will find that most people do own credit cards. Some of them also have many credit cards. Everybody seems to own one. So why can't you?

Although credit cards offer you many benefits, the most important of them all is the convenience which you are given. The sole and the prime reason for getting a credit card will be because of its convenience. A few years back, when not many accepted credit cards this was not a good choice. But in today's world it is quite convenient to own one. Carrying lots of money on you might be unsafe as well as inconvenient. This is when a credit card which is a small piecemade of plastic can be very attractive. You will not need to keep paying the bills till the next months billing cycle. So buying when you want is possible even if you don't have ready cash on you. A great reason to apply for a credit card is that you can buy now and then pay them later. Merchants also offer you an installment payment plan which is interest free that is when you can make a very big purchase and keep paying it off in regular installments. Hence credit cards work as long term loans. You will be also entitled to discounts on your shopping with credit cards. Tie ups are made between the merchants and the credit card companies. These are indeed quite a lot of benefits that a credit card can offer.

There are many methods in applying for a credit card. You can either do it over the phone (by getting the representative to make an appointment with you), the net or applying it in person. A lot of representatives will be asking you to apply with their company. To get a credit card you will need to fill an application form which will be quite easy as you will have an assistant in guiding you. By filling this form you will be agreeing on all their conditions as this form is actually an agreement form. You will receive your credit card as soon as this is done and your credits are checked by the company you signed with.

It is not a compulsion for you to apply for one. But for most people who do not have a credit card, it is highly recommended you apply for one as soon as possible.

Making a Good Credit Card Comparison

Many people are into the fray for the need for a credit card for some reason or the other. It is also a well known fact that before choosing a particular card you need to do enough research and make enough enquiries. But what many are not aware of is how to make a credit card comparison which is very important in deciding on the best card.

How To Find The Best Credit Card?

Today the market is filled with companies that are ready to offer cards to people and in order to attract customers they make many attractive offers. As a customer it is your duty to conduct complete research and find out how authentic and useful these offers are. In order to compare cards you can check online ratings given to card companies. These ratings are based on many findings and therefore you can trust them to make decisions.

On the net you can also find sites that are put up by other banks and financial institutions in order to help customers to get necessary information on companies offering credit cards. These sites also provide the facility of getting rates from other companies which facilitates comparison. They also give details of card deals that are offered by the companies and the most popular one being the 0 interest cards that are very helpful to customers.

What You Need To Be Careful About?

Making a choice of the credit card is very difficult due the presence of numerous credit card companies. Your choice should also depend on the use of the card in your special fiscal situation because there are many cards that serve different purposes. If you are aware of that then you can choose the right one easily. One type of card that is very popular these days is the card that allows transfer of balance from one card to the other. This card is very popular because of the amount of money that can be saved by the user. The facility is also offered by the low interest credit cards. These cards facilitate savings and therefore people prefer to subscribe to such cards.

With the fierce competition that exists among the many companies, it is interesting to view the offers and then make a choice as most of them are at par when it comes to the facilities offered. All you need to do is to keep your eyes open to all the available information regarding the benefits and offers offered by the companies and you are bound to get a card that suits you best.

This form of awareness and caution is necessary, failing which you could get a card with minimum offer and maximum charge and you could be stuck with it for life. Making good credit card comparison helps a lot in benefiting from a card that is more of an asset. After all it is your savings that are going to be affected by the purchase.

The Benefits Of Accessing Credit Reports On A Regular Basis

Credit and debt have become the norm. If you were to look around your neighborhood and take stock of the homes and cars people have you may think that you are living in a prosperous age. In actuality, most properties and vehicles today are not bought outright, they are obtained through loans and lines of credit.

Every individual has a credit rating and report. Though this information is not usually seen by consumers, it is always analyzed by lenders prior to the granting of a financial service. If your report was to contain information of a somewhat negative nature, this will have a serious impact on your ability to acquire loans and related services.

By accessing your personal credit report, you can take stock of your current standing. Not only would this allow you to understand how easy it will be to be granted a new loan, you can also ensure that your identity is not being used for fraud. Unfortunately, many people fall victim of ID fraud and are unaware of the problem until they apply for a loan or similar service and are refused due to unexpected bad credit.

By regularly monitoring the information kept on file in relation to your financial standing and monetary obligations, you can help reduce the risk of falling victim to ID theft. What's more, there is always the possibility of creditors and lenders making mistakes. By going to the effort to read all the entries in your report you can ensure that you are not going to be viewed unfavorably unnecessarily.

If you are to request a report to be sent to you, you will need to know how to properly analyze the data that it contains. Most feature four sections: personal information, score, account history, and inquiry information. Each section contains valuable entries and should be checked carefully. If you are concerned about fraud, the account history gives an indication of the different loans and agreements that have been taken out in your name.

A personal credit report is a document that everyone should access at least once a year. No matter what your current financial situation is, regularly checking the financial account information that is held on you can help combat identify theft and also allow you to make informed decisions in relation to applying for loans and similar services. Though there is usually a small fee involved with accessing a report, it is money well spent.

Rebuild Your Credit With A Prepaid Credit Card

It can be pretty tough when your credit is bad and it is next to impossible to get credit when you need it. Most major credit card companies will not talk to you, and a lender - well, forget about it. There is a way, though, out of the tough situation with a prepaid credit card. Here is what you can do with a prepaid credit card to help rebuild your credit score.

Need A Bad Credit Rating

One of the best things about a prepaid credit card is that it was designed for people with bad credit. In fact, that is one of the qualifications. There will not be any check on your credit rating, or your employment. Anyone can get one of these credit cards, but you will need to deposit a cash amount equal to the credit limit you want. This lets you know that it operates on a debit basis - no actual credit is given.

Get A Card That Reports To A Credit Bureau

Not many prepaid credit cards actually report to a credit bureau. That is, however, the kind of card that you want to get. While others make having cash handy, it really will not help you (or anyone with bad credit) in the long run.

Watch The Fees

Prepaid credit cards often come with a number of fees. You should compare one card with another in order to get the fewest fees. In order to get a prepaid credit card that reports to a credit bureau, you will probably have to pay an annual fee - could be as high as $100.

Look For Benefits

Most prepaid cards do not come with any benefits, but some do. You can get points, like on a regular credit card, that are useable for a few benefits - like free phone time, and more.

No Credit Card Abuse

Another good thing about these credit cards is that you can never go over your limit, or have to pay any late fees or interest. (Hey, this is sounding better all the time). This means that if it reports to a credit bureau, that it would be impossible to get a lower score than what you may already have with this kind of card.

Easily Put Cash On Your Card

Most prepaid cards will allow you to easily put credit on it from just about anywhere. You can even put your paycheck onto it by Direct Deposit.

Use It Like A Credit Card

A number of these prepaid credit cards can be used in the same way as a credit card. You can set up automatic bill payments, purchase things online, or over the phone. If you want this feature, however, be sure that the ad says that you can do this.

Like any other credit card, you will want to compare features and fees in order to find the best prepaid credit card for your needs. While most of them are similar, the fees vary widely. Since no qualifications are needed, why not get the best?

Help Find The Best Credit Cards Rates By Researching Credit Cards Comparison

If you have been turned down for credit in the past and you want to be able to get financing to buy something. We help show people how to compare different offers to find the best credit card to fit their needs. Depending on why you are looking for a credit card. You need to first learn about the benefits that you can pick from based on what is important to you.

Your credit score is the primary factor that determines what kind of credit card deal you can get approved for. There is a way to repair your credit just by disputing all the negative things that are on your credit report. You would be surprised at how easy credit repair is. All you have to do a lot of times is just initiate a dispute about any bad item on your credit report. If they don't address your request within 30 days then it has to be removed from your credit report legally. This doesn't matter if the information is true or not. Most of the time that is all it takes to get bad items removed from your credit report.

Your personal credit report is your property you have the right to dispute information on that report that can be used against you. This helps you get a better deal when doing credit cards comparison. The credit bureaus want you to have bad credit. The lower your credit score is the more money the banks make when they lend money to you. All these institutions work together. So this means you are guilty of any and all information that is reported about you to them until you prove your innocence. The problem is no one tells you that you even have this right to repair your credit. It is not to the best interest of the credit bureaus or the banks that lend money to hand out this information.

If you want a new credit card then you will want to look at the benefits of the card that you want. You can choose from things like low interest credit cards, balance transfer credit cards, cash back credit cards, bad credit credit cards, and much more. Look through our guide for credit cards comparison to find out what kind of credit card you would like to have.

Credit cards are a great tool when financing things that you need. They are no good to you if all you plan on doing is shopping for things that you can't afford. This is what gets people in trouble as most of us know all to well. Now if you are financing just 1 large purchase that you want to make payments on. Using a credit card for that would be a smart thing to do. Or if you just want to earn rewards on things that you need to buy regularly like buying gas. You need good credit to get approved for these kinds of credit card offers. So if your credit isn't that great and you want to repair it. Check out our guide for easy credit repair. This will give you more information on how you can raise your credit score so you can get approved for these kinds of credit card offers.

Is it Possible to Improve Your Credit Scores and Live a Normal Life?

A low credit score can really be bothersome when you need to rent a home, get an installment loan, or just about any type of loan. Creditors usually look at your credit report and if your it is below the ideal 660, they will tend to reject your application. The worse news is that this rejection is still another reason for your score to sink further.

If your whole financial world revolves around credit cards and loans, you have to realize that your credit score is the bottom line of all your financial transactions. It affects how much interests you pay on your cards. It also determines the amount of money you have to pay on your other bills wherever you may work or live in this country. It makes sense these days to improve your financial standing Failing to do so will greatly reduce your chances of getting advantageous interest rates. Your score is reviewed by loan companies and banks before they allow you to get hold of their money. A low score means higher interests. If you need to get a loan for a car or have to get home insurance, or even a cell phone service, a high credit score will get you lower premium payments and a better package for services you require. Even landlords can check your finances, as well as employers before accepting a prospective employee.

So how do you improve your credit standing and still live a normal life? It would seem that you will always be under scrutiny every time you transact where credit or loans are involved. Borrowing and loans are a privilege but you need to use them properly to benefit from it. By setting your mind firmly on this belief, you can begin to improve your credit rating slowly but surely.

For most people, their first credit card is the genesis of their credit history. This is good because a longer credit history is a plus when calculating your scores. However, applying for many credit cards can actually lower your score since each credit inquiry will cost you up to five points. It may seem like a good idea to get a card from a company that will not report your credit limit to the established credit bureaus or doesn't give you a spending limit but this is actually a sure way to hurt your credit score. If you already have several cards, don't cancel them all at one time. Doing so can lower the credit available to you and deduct points from your credit score. Try to keep old credit cards and use them from time to time in order to maintain a long credit history which can help a lot to improve your credit scores. And keeping your credit card balance lower than 30% of your credit limit will also be a great help.

All credit gurus are unanimous in saying that paying your debt always on time is the best way to improve your credit scores. One late payment is all it takes to ruin your credit score - a deduction of as much as 100 points and it stays on your credit report for seven long years.

Books by the same Author:

Search: "Harrison Moore"
at Amazon

Kind reader,

Thank you very much, I hope you enjoyed the book.

Can I ask you a big favor?

I would be grateful if you would please take a few minutes to leave me a gold star on Amazon.

Thank you again for your support.

Harrison Moore

www.ingramcontent.com/pod-product-compliance
Lightning Source LLC
Chambersburg PA
CBHW071409210526
45465CB00001B/303